I0139718

THE DARK ARTS FOR BEGINNERS

Nick Robideau

BROADWAY PLAY PUBLISHING INC
New York
www.broadwayplaypublishing.com
info@broadwayplaypublishing.com

THE DARK ARTS FOR BEGINNERS
© Copyright 2022 Nick Robideau

First edition: September 2022
I S B N: 978-0-88145-944-9

Book design: Marie Donovan
Page make-up: Adobe InDesign
Typeface: Palatino

THE DARK ARTS FOR BEGINNERS was developed in part at the Lanford Wilson New American Play Festival (Kitt Lavoie, Artistic Director; Kenneth L Stilson, Executive Director).

CHARACTERS & SETTING

EVA, *17 years old. Awkward, earnest, and very unsure of herself. Feels and cares about things very deeply. Wants very badly to fit in and be liked but isn't quite sure how to do it.*

JANE, *18 years old. EVA's older sister. Droll, dry, and often seems exasperated by EVA, but just barely under the surface, she loves her sister very fiercely.*

ASHANTI, *17 years old. EVA's friend and crush. She has a deeply felt but very teenage sense of spirituality and often takes herself a little too seriously.*

IMOGEN, *17 years old. EVA's frenemy. The cool kid who makes a great show of always being snarky, rude, and above everything, but is secretly smarter and more sensitive than she lets on.*

CLAIRE, *17 years old. IMOGEN's best friend and sidekick. Very nervous and neurotic. She sometimes seems like a bit of a doormat, especially with IMOGEN, but she can be stronger than she seems when she really wants to be.*

CERNUNNOS, *An ancient god. He appears as a disembodied voice, then a shadow, then as a 30-something suburban dad. In his initial forms, he's intense and foreboding, but also slightly ridiculous in his self-importance. In his dad form, he's corny and nurturing, with some of that foreboding quality still simmering under the surface.*

Time: The year 2057

Place: A basement somewhere in suburbia

Scene 1

(A semi-finished basement. Wood paneled walls, bare concrete floor with a couple of dusty area rugs, fluorescent light bulbs on the drop ceiling, currently turned off. Lighting is provided by a number of candles scattered around the space. Upstage center, a small table—or maybe even just a stack of boxes—covered in a red tablecloth, with a purple placemat over it. On top of the placemat are four more candles, a figurine of a black cat, a bowl of water, a knife, a stick of burning incense, and, in the center of it all, a pentagram that's been roughly cut out of cardboard. A circle is formed by plant stands, deeply scratched cat towers, and other random objects. Five figures, all wearing dark robes, stand inside that circle: ASHANTI, 17, who enthusiastically beats out a tribal rhythm on a hand drum; IMOGEN, 17, who periodically sighs and theatrically rolls her eyes; CLAIRE, 17, who watches the proceedings very intently, occasionally mouths words to herself, and fidgets nervously; JANE, 18, who slouches and looks bored; and EVA, 17, who leads the circle, occasionally consulting an electronic device that's something like an iPad, but not quite.)

EVA:
Here us now, all ye Gods of old
In our time of great need
Under skies that cry out for your purification
Putrid and boiling with our collective human stain
We draw down your power
We beg of you to cleanse our Earth

To open thy...thy...um...
Sorry guys, the thing is—the screen is frozen.

JANE: Smack it.

(IMOGEN *snickers*.)

EVA: What?

JANE: You have to smack it when it does that.

(EVA *smacks the side of the device.*)

EVA: Oh. Okay.
To open thy sacred eyes and hands
And guide us back to the path of the Mother
Cleanse now our land, sea, and sky
Save us from the fate that our fellow man has forced
   upon us
Keepers of the sacred watchtowers
Tis time to tend to your duties
Alight, and to your places!

(Long pause)

EVA: I said...to your places! As in, places everyone. Go,
take the candles!

(IMOGEN, JANE, *and* CLAIRE *walk toward the altar to collect
their candles.* ASHANTI *twirls towards the altar, drumming
even more intently and vocalizing wordlessly.)*

ASHANTI: *(Singing)* Ooooh, behold the sacred flames of
tiiiime.

EVA: *(Through clenched teeth)* That's not in the script,
Ashanti.

(ASHANTI *stops twirling.*)

ASHANTI: Oh. Sorry. I just got caught up in the
moment. Is that going to—is that going to make it not
work? Do we have to start over?

IMOGEN: Oh Jesus Christ, please no.

EVA: I told you! No invoking non-pagan deities in the circle. It's not respectful.

IMOGEN: Sorry. *(Beat)* Oh Corn Mother, please no. Better?

EVA: Yes. Thank you. And we don't have to start over—though we really should because of Imogen. But we all have to stick with the script, you guys.

ASHANTI: Sorry. Sorry, Eva.

EVA: And that's enough drumming for now. But the enthusiasm is really, really appreciated. All around.

(EVA *smiles at* ASHANTI, *who blushes.*)

ASHANTI: Thanks.

(EVA *collects herself and looks down at the device again.*)

EVA:
I banish thee, all forces of foulness and corruption
Make way for ye goodness and light of old
Heed the solemn words of the keepers

(EVA *hands the device to* CLAIRE, *who startles and nearly drops it.*)

CLAIRE: Oh God. I mean goddess. I—I—I don't think I can.

EVA: Come on, Claire. This is the future of the whole planet. We're all counting on you.

IMOGEN: Yeah, no pressure or anything.

(CLAIRE *takes a breath, looks down at the device, and shouts the following at a rapid clip.*)

CLAIRE:
I call to the watchtower of the East
Hear me, ancient spirits of Air
Banish all the toxic vapors that fill you
And replace them with the sweet breaths of old

(CLAIRE *practically throws the device at* ASHANTI. ASHANTI *takes a deep, dramatic, cleansing breath, then begins reading with great gravitas, as if giving a sermon.*)

ASHANTI: I…call to the watchTOWER…of the South Heeaaar me, oh ancient SPIRITS…of fire!

(*Long pause*)

IMOGEN: Some time this year.

ASHANTI: It…it froze again.

IMOGEN: How old is that stupid CRAD, anyhow, Jane? It looks like some shit from the Thirties.

JANE: Hey, it's not my fault Eva dropped hers in the trash cuber last night. She's lucky I'm letting her borrow mine.

EVA: (*Under her breath to Jane*) Do NOT talk down to me in front of the coven. I'm the high priestess! You're always talking down to me…

JANE: (*Under her breath*) And here I thought I was dropping everything to help you out. Without a thank you. As usual.

ASHANTI: So, um, the CRAD is still…

JANE: Yeah, you have to—

ASHANTI: Right, right.

(ASHANTI *smacks the side of the device, which we now know is called a CRAD.*)

ASHANTI:
Take thy heat that burdens us all
The oppressing sun, the fevered tendrils
And lift it away with cooler tidings

(ASHANTI *holds her hands out, the CRAD in one, and lifts them up dramatically.* JANE *plucks the device from her hands and reads from it in a warp speed, mumbly monotone.*)

JANE:
I call to the watchtower of the West
Hear me, oh spirits of water
Banish the oil and other foul fluids that have harmed
    us so
And call back home the ever rising seas

(JANE *thrusts the CRAD into* IMOGEN's *hand. She stares at it.*)

IMOGEN: Do I really have to do this?

JANE: If I have to do it, then so do you.

ASHANTI: Imogen, I just have to—ugh, I just have to say it. Your negative attitude about this is really killing my spiritual high.

IMOGEN: You want a spiritual high? Go huff paint thinner like a normal kid.

EVA: You guys, really. This is not at all respectful to the ancient Watchtowers.

CLAIRE: Eva's right. These are very powerful forces we're dealing with here. We...oh man...we don't even really understand the true extent of what we're trying to tap into, which I've tried to say to all of you from the very beginning. At the least, at the very least, we need to do exactly what the book told us to do, and that means sticking to the script. Please.

IMOGEN: You do realize that just by saying that, you're going off script.

CLAIRE: Oh. Oh no. I'm sorry. I'm so sorry.

IMOGEN: Who are you even apologizing to? And why are you taking Eva's side?

CLAIRE: I'm not! You're right. Obviously. This is all completely lame and stupid.

IMOGEN: You said, and I quote, "Eva's right."

CLAIRE: I don't know. I'm just—feeling a little overwhelmed by all this. My anxiety's all over the place. I don't even know what I'm saying. And this week has just / been—

IMOGEN: I say this because I love you, but just get meds already like the rest of us.

EVA: Imogen, please. Come on. We can't do this without the North. It's the grounding element.

IMOGEN: Ugh.

JANE: The sooner you just say it, the sooner this is going to be over.

IMOGEN: Fine!
I call to the watchtower of the North
Hear me, oh spirits of Earth
Cast out the terrible toxins of the goodly soil *(Beat)*
"Goodly"? Really Eva?

(EVA gives IMOGEN a look of death.)

IMOGEN: Okay, sure.
And…ground us in your ancient wisdom.

(EVA takes the CRAD from IMOGEN.)

EVA:
And now, with the watchtowers steeling our spirits
And the strength of Air, Fire, Water, and Earth to
    fortify us
We turn to the Earth Mother, the ancient Crone
This coven calls upon your awesome power
To set things back to how they once were
Blessed Be!

(Pause)

EVA: Ahem. I said—Blessed Be!

ALL: Blessed Be.

EVA: And now, join hands everyone. Come on, do it.

(Everyone joins hands except IMOGEN. *A beat, then Imogen sighs and does it too.)*

EVA: Feel the ancient vibrations rising from the earth, up into you feet, through your body, and finally, let it reach your voice, like this.…

*(*EVA *plants her feet, closes her eyes, hums, then vocalizes on an "ah". After a moment of this,* IMOGEN *breaks the circle.)*

IMOGEN: Okay, I'm sorry but what is even the point of all this?

ASHANTI: Eva told us a thousand times. It's a traditional healing ritual, but focused out, to the whole planet.

IMOGEN: Yeah, because scientists and politicians and whatever couldn't fix the planet in like 80 years of trying, but ten minutes of chanting and humming, that should do it.

ASHANTI: Then why are you even here?

IMOGEN: I thought it might be good for a laugh. I was wrong. I'm bored shitless.

JANE: Please. Just hum or whatever so we can get on with it already. I'm missing the Bleeding Arteries show for this.

EVA: Everyone, please, please, please just stick to the script. *The Dark Arts for Beginners*—the book—it says it's super important that we focus our energy on the task at hand.

IMOGEN: Oh Jesus Christ. "The book says. The book says." The book was published in like 1995. That's older than my mom. Who cares about some outdated Twentieth Century bullshit?

CLAIRE: I don't know. Maybe we shouldn't…tempt fate.

IMOGEN: Seriously, Claire?

CLAIRE: But I mean, this is all completely Eva's fault for getting us into this outdated Twentieth Century bullshit in the first place. Obviously. Imogen is totally right.

ASHANTI: You don't have to just agree with everything Imogen says all the time, Claire. Listen to your first impulse. Being your own person can be a beautiful thing.

IMOGEN: Oh my God. Just because your parents are therapists, doesn't mean you're enlightened or whatever. Do you even know what half the stuff you say actually means?

ASHANTI: I know it feels safer to project your—

EVA: Ash!

ASHANTI: Hm?

EVA: You can do the drums now.

ASHANTI: Oh—yay!

EVA: Everyone else, reform the circle.

(JANE *sighs and takes* EVA's *hand.* IMOGEN *just glares.* CLAIRE *looks hesitantly at* IMOGEN.)

EVA: Imogen—please? You can talk all the shit you want later. I'll owe you big, I promise.

(IMOGEN *sighs, then hums, puts one hand in* CLAIRE's, *and the other in* JANE's. JANE *and* EVA *complete the circle.* EVA *again hums and vocalizes on "ah".* IMOGEN *makes a face, then does the same.* CLAIRE *follows suit. Then* ASHANTI. *Then* JANE)

EVA: Move in a counterclockwise…no, um, clockwise….yeah, clockwise circle, while you continue channeling the earth's healing energy.

(*Through the following,* ASHANTI *drums faster and faster. As she does, the rest of the group circles faster and faster.*)

EVA:
I invoke thee, oh ancient ones
You're our last hope
Unknowable forces of Cernunnos and Ceridwen
Only you can save this once-blue orb
Okay, now keep circling, and repeat everyone:
We conjure thee

ALL: We conjure thee

EVA: We conjure thee!

ALL: We conjure thee!

EVA: WE CONJURE THEE!!!

ALL: WE CONJURE THEE!!!

*(A piercing siren sounds, somewhere outside. CLAIRE
screams and stops in her tracks. ASHANTI stops drumming.
A chain reaction as the whole group goes down like
dominos.)*

IMOGEN: Fucking hell, Claire!

CLAIRE: Sorry. I…panicked. I'm never going to get used
to that.

*(The siren goes off again as they pick themselves up off the
ground.)*

ASHANTI: Couldn't they make it a nice soothing voice
saying "Time to get inside, everyone. Time to get
inside." I don't get why it has to be an ear-splitting
doomsday siren.

IMOGEN: Well it kind of is doomsday, so…

*(JANE reaches over and turns on the overhead lights.
ASHANTI, CLAIRE, and IMOGEN walk over to a coat
rack, previously hidden by shadows, and start donning
increasingly elaborate protective gear: masks, face shields,
gloves that zip to their sleeves, hats with fabric that connects
to their jackets.)*

EVA: But the ritual's not over!

IMOGEN: Siren went off, Eva. Fifteen minutes to curfew.

EVA: This curfew is bullshit. You said so yourself.

IMOGEN: So is this stupid ritual. And I'm not going to get docked points off next month's rations for skipping out on it, so curfew wins.

EVA: Claire! We're talking about the ancient powers of the occult here. We have to do it right.

CLAIRE: I know, I know, and if it's any consolation, I'm going to have nightmares about the possible consequences for a week. I don't think the curfew is bullshit, though, and given the choice between being cooked like a baked potato, and maybe annoying some archaic gods, I'll go with the less upsetting option.

EVA: But—

(CLAIRE *has taken a CRAD from her jacket pocket and puts it in* EVA*'s face.*)

CLAIRE: Look—the U V warning for today is eighteen. That's a code purple, Eva. Purple!

IMOGEN: The color coding system is just a government tool to keep obsessive-compulsive sheep like you afraid and compliant.

CLAIRE: I know, but—there's also a real reason behind all of it. Really bad things can happen if you get too much light or too much air.

(IMOGEN *edges towards the door.*)

IMOGEN: Oh no, oh shit…you're right. Something's happening. I feel something…burning. Could it be the air, or could it just be chlamydia? Better test it out…

(IMOGEN *edges closer to the door.*)

CLAIRE: Imogen, come on! This isn't a joke. Don't stand so close to the door without your face shield on. Please…

IMOGEN: I think my nose is melting off. Heeeelp meee..…

CLAIRE: It's not funny!

IMOGEN: Lighten up. Jeez.

CLAIRE: Lighten up? We all have a seventy-five percent chance of getting at least one of either skin cancer or lung cancer by the age of fifty. There's nothing funny about that. Nothing.

IMOGEN: And what can I do about that? Nothing.

EVA: You can come back and finish the ritual!

IMOGEN: Shut up, dweeb. I can't do anything REAL about it except have a good time for as long as I can. So fuck all of you for messing with that. Especially you, Claire.

CLAIRE: Me?

IMOGEN: I don't expect any better from those two hippy dippy losers. And Jane, you're doing the devoted big sister act here but are so clearly not feeling it, so we're cool. But you, Claire, you're supposed to be my best friend. You're suppose to get me.

CLAIRE: I'm sorry. I'm sorry. I know I'm super lame and annoying. I know. I just…worry. Please, just put on your face shield? I'll feel a lot better. Please?

(IMOGEN *puts on her face shield.*)

IMOGEN: Can we go now?

ASHANTI: Hang on. Wait up for me.

EVA: Ash—not you, too?

ASHANTI: I am so appreciative of this time together, Eva. Really. It's been beautiful. It's been healing. But my dad is going to kill me if I don't get in before the sun comes up. I'm sorry.

EVA: But—but—this is the future of the whole world, ladies! This is our last chance! I mean, this is it, you realize that? The quarantine regulations are permanent now. We're never going to see the sun on the grass again, or—or birds. Or, I don't know, see a rainbow.

IMOGEN: Cool, thanks for the pep talk, coach.

CLAIRE: To be fair, there weren't a lot of birds left anyhow. Or grass…

ASHANTI: We got through most of the ritual. Maybe that was enough to do something. I know I felt my spirit move.

EVA: You did? Really?

ASHANTI: Absolutely.

IMOGEN: Quit flirting and come ON, Ash!

(ASHANTI *smiles, puts on the last of her protective gear, and moves to join* IMOGEN *and* CLAIRE. EVA *suddenly picks up a book from the floor. It reads "The Dark Arts for Beginners".)*

EVA: Oh no. Wait! Oh crap. We have to at least close the magic circle. That's the most important part! Come back! *(She picks up the knife from the table.)* Just get back to your watchtower positions. I'll hold out the sacred blade, and you'll all—

IMOGEN: Be real. The sacred blade is a butter knife from your mom's silverware drawer.

EVA: So?

IMOGEN: So none of this shit actually matters. Sorry, but it doesn't.

(EVA *leafs through pages in the book.)*

EVA: But the book says…the book says if we don't close the circle, the door between worlds will remain open, and unwanted forces could come in. Unwanted forces!

CLAIRE: Maybe we need to do it, Imogen. That sounds bad.

IMOGEN: At this point, we're all going to have to run to make curfew. Literally run. I've seen you in phys ed. Prospects aren't looking good here.

CLAIRE: Have fun closing the door for us. Bye Eva!

(All three exit. ASHANTI *waves as she goes.)*

EVA: Shit. Shit.

JANE: Just close the door or circle or whatever it is yourself. What's the big deal?

*(*EVA *furiously turns pages in the book.)*

EVA: Okay. Let me just see…great. Wonderful.

JANE: What are you freaking out about?

EVA: By leaving the circle before it was closed, they tore holes in it.

JANE: Okay…?

EVA: So it's too late. The veil between the worlds has been ruptured. It's not even worth trying to close it now. Whatever any of that actually means.

JANE: Cool, so that means we're done?

EVA: Yeah, we're done. You can go watch your concert or whatever. Obligation fulfilled.

JANE: Great. I mean, it's probably half over by now, but thanks for the permission.

*(*JANE *moves towards the stairs.* EVA *looks down at the floor and kicks at the altar.)*

EVA: Stupid. Stupid stupid stupid stupid.…

*(*JANE *sighs and turns back around.)*

JANE: Hey. Hey, look at me.

EVA: Don't you want to go catch your concert?

JANE: Whatever. They'll probably do another reunion show…someday. Now look at me.

(EVA *looks up at* JANE.)

EVA: Ugh. Fine.

JANE: Your feet are on the ground.

EVA: My feet are on the ground.

JANE: Your body's in this space.

EVA: My body's in this space.

JANE: Pick something in the room to focus on, listen to my voice, and breathe in, and out. In, and out. In, and out. *(Beat)* Better?

EVA: I was so stupid to think any of this was a good idea.

JANE: For whatever it's worth, I don't think you're stupid.

EVA: That's the kind of thing big sisters have to say. You don't actually mean it.

JANE: I do. It's really and truly impressive that you wrote all that yourself. Plus, it took everyone's mind off all the other crap that's going on, at least for a little while. She'll never admit it, but I think deep down, even Imogen appreciates that.

EVA: Well, thanks and all…but why couldn't you say all that in front of everyone else?

JANE: Hey, don't get too greedy with my good will. You're talking to the watchtower of the west here. I've got an image to maintain.

EVA: I'm serious. Why can't you actually support me when it counts?

(JANE glares at EVA.)

JANE: Yeah, Okay. I'm going to give you a minute by yourself to think about just how unfair that is. And hey, maybe I'll still catch the encore of the Arteries show, if I'm lucky. *(She shakes her head and exits upstairs.)*

EVA: I'm sorry, you're right, I'm a jerk. Jane? I'm sorry! *(Pause)* Shit…

(EVA sighs, slowly, sadly extinguishes the candles, packs up her altar, and puts all the basement furniture and detritus back in place. She takes a look around her, sighs, and sullenly walks back upstairs, tuning off the overhead lights as she does. A moment of darkness on stage—and then, a pair of red eyes begins glowing in the darkness.)

Scene 2

(The next day—or night, really. The same partially finished basement. EVA and ASHANTI both sit cross-legged on a yoga mat, with the altar cloth between them. It's laden with candles and other various objects—some from the previous day's ritual, some different. ASHANTI holds a small stone and studies it very intently.)

EVA: That one's agate.

ASHANTI: I've never seen anything like it before.

EVA: Actually it's pretty common. Relatively speaking. I still like it, though.

(ASHANTI closes one eye and holds the stone up to the other eye.)

ASHANTI: You can see through it, just a little. It like that place you told me about—the hazy veil between worlds. *(She looks at her own hand through the stone.)*

EVA: Agate's just supposed to be for happiness and good health. Nothing fancy or really powerful. Honestly, I just wanted to have another crystal on the altar and it's what I could find.

ASHANTI: I'm feeling happier and healthier already. It must be working.

EVA: That'd be a first.

ASHANTI: Okay, ouch.

EVA: What? No. Oh shit, no. I mean for any of this working. I don't...you're pretty much the happiest and healthiest person I know. Even now. I mean, it's honestly kind of confusing. *(Beat)* In a good way.

ASHANTI: You found the inspiration inside yourself to put all this together. Maybe you're not as confused as you think.

EVA: But I kind of am. I mean, it didn't work, right?

ASHANTI: You don't know that. It's barely been a day.

EVA: It was just like—I can suddenly see myself through their eyes. My sister. Claire. Imogen. Oh man, Imogen. And I just...I look so dumb.

ASHANTI: You were so excited about all this. I hope you don't lose that.

EVA: That's the thing. I just wanted to do something. Anything. Or just...feel like I was doing something. But that was stupid. All I did was spend like a weekend reading some book and a few hours writing that ritual. That's...pathetic.

ASHANTI: Can you see yourself through my eyes?

EVA: What?

ASHANTI: You can see yourself through Imogen and Jane and Claire's eyes. What about me?

EVA: No. You're different.

ASHANTI: Different how?

EVA: You're way too nice. And in my head, because I'm pretty much a trash person, I start to think—well Ashanti can't actually be that nice and that positive and that peaceful, not really, nobody can be, so she must secretly be thinking all these horrible thoughts at all times. She must actually be the meanest one out of all of us, deep down. Oh shit. Sorry. I shouldn't have said that.

ASHANTI: Don't apologize. Honesty is beautiful in all of its forms. I appreciate it.

EVA: Of course you do. *(Beat)* Wait. How DO you see me? *(Beat)* Don't tell me if it's bad. *(Beat)* Okay, do tell me if it's bad, but…make it quick.

ASHANTI: Before, up to now, I didn't see anything. It's like you weren't there. You were…negative space.

EVA: I should mention that I don't necessarily think honesty is beautiful, at least not in all its forms, so.…

ASHANTI: Hang on, I wasn't done. Once you found the book, and wrote the ritual, and started explaining it all to us, and found your true voice at that altar…it was like some kind of inner light in you found its way out. I swear, your eyes looked different. They were brighter. I feel like I'm seeing you—really seeing you—for the first time.

EVA: Wow. Okay. Um…sorry. I don't know what to say.

ASHANTI: Tell me about your favorite thing on the altar.

(EVA thinks for a moment, and picks up another stone.)

EVA: This is called "The Ice of Eternity".

(EVA hands the stone to ASHANTI.)

ASHANTI: The Ice of Eternity…wow…

EVA: If it was gray it would be used for centering ourselves within our own bodies. Rose would be for stimulating love. But the clear quartz, that's about helping us connect to the spirit of the natural world. To really tap into the universal life forces, you know?

ASHANTI: Oh my goddess…

EVA: What? What?

ASHANTI: I think I feel it.

EVA: Oh—are you…are you okay?

ASHANTI: Not me—the crystal. It's—oh wow. I think it's heating up. Yeah it's definitely heating up. And I feel it, like, sort of pulsing. This is amazing.

EVA: I don't—hang on, let me see if the book says anything / about—

ASHANTI: Just be in the moment, Eva. Here.

(ASHANTI *places her palm in* EVA*'s, with the crystal squeezed between them. There is, in fact, a low humming in the air. A vibration.* EVA *blushes.*)

ASHANTI: Do you feel it?

(*Pause. The humming gets louder.* EVA *does feel something, but she's not sure what, exactly.*)

EVA: It's definitely…warm.

(*A moment. They look at each other. The humming sound is now unmistakable.* EVA *and* ASHANTI *look around them.*)

ASHANTI: (*Softly*) We invoke thee, ancient ones…

(*A sudden crack, and the lights go out.* EVA *screams.*)

EVA: Shit shit shit shit…

JANE: (*O S. Calling from upstairs*) Flip the switches, Eva!

EVA: What?

JANE: (*O S*) I think Mom blew a fuse again. Flip the stupid switches!

EVA: Oh, um…

(A moment, then the lights come back on. EVA is standing at a fuse box down stage right of the altar. ASHANTI sits serenely, smiling. Upstage, and unseen by either of them, is a large shadow of a figure with stag-like horns.)

ASHANTI: I think this might be the most amazing thing to ever happen to me. I feel changed by this.

EVA: I mean, not to be a wet blanket or anything, but my mom probably plugged in her flat iron and the air decarbonator at the same time again.

ASHANTI: You felt it. I know you felt it.

(EVA sits back down next to ASHANTI.)

EVA: Do you really believe all this stuff? One hundred percent, in your heart believe it?

ASHANTI: I believe in creation instead of destruction. Healing instead of harm. That's the code I live my life by. All this magic stuff? In the end it doesn't really matter if the magic or the ritual or the crystal or any of that is actually real. What matters is that we were trying to create and heal. That's all I care about.

EVA: Creation instead of destruction. Healing instead of harm. That's a beautiful code.

ASHANTI: It helps to keep things simple. Whenever I'm not sure what to say or how to act, I think about the code, and I always know, right away.

EVA: I wish Jane and Claire and Imogen had a code. Maybe they'd understand what I was trying to do. *(Beat)* Imogen barely looked at me at school. I think she hates me now.

ASHANTI: Imogen hates everyone.

EVA: Oh God—I was just saying that. You think she really does hate me?

ASHANTI: Who cares if she does?

EVA: No you're right. You're completely right. *(Beat)* But seriously—does Imogen hate me?

ASHANTI: I think she might feel threatened that you took charge. But I seriously doubt she hates you.

EVA: I have to try to do something to balance out my image with her. Something really cool. Yesterday she said she'd rather be huffing paint thinner. Where would I get some of that?

ASHANTI: Why did you do this—to save the planet, or to make Imogen like you?

EVA: Maybe—a little of both?

ASHANTI: Oh, Eva. You have to get out of that mindset.

EVA: I just—I miss us sometimes, you know? The way you, me and Claire used to be. The three amigas. The three musketeers!

ASHANTI: I don't think we ever actually called ourselves that…

EVA: I did. In my head. Just go with it. Then Imogen just waltzed in and screwed up everything.

ASHANTI: She was a climate refugee, Eva. She lost everything in the Great California Fire of '52. Including her father. Remember?

EVA: I know, and that's super sad. I'm not saying it isn't. But—it doesn't change the fact that she stole Claire.

ASHANTI: We still see Claire all the time.

EVA: It's not the same. And even you and me don't do everything together like we used to. Imogen just—she ruined the whole dynamic.

ASHANTI: I've been working on my spiritual practice. It's very solitary stuff. And besides, Imogen moved

here in seventh grade. Relationships change at that age.
It's only natural.

EVA: Okay, but....

ASHANTI: Why are you changing the subject? All that
stuff with Imogen and Claire is ancient history. I care
about the here and now. Eva. We shared something
with the Ice of Eternity. You know we did.

EVA: No, I—you're right. You're totally right. I just…
get in my head sometimes, I guess.

ASHANTI: About Imogen?

EVA: Not just about Imogen. Maybe it's just easier to
talk about that part of things.

ASHANTI: What's the other part?

EVA: The part that's not so easy, hence the not talking.

*(A loaded pause. JANE appears at the top of the stairs and
quietly watches. Her back is to the shadow of the antlered
figure, and she doesn't see it.)*

ASHANTI: I can respect that. Sometimes silence says
more than words can. *(She picks up a small bottle from the
altar.)*

EVA: That's an essential oil.

ASHANTI: I know. You already showed me. *(She dabs
some on each finger.)*

EVA: The way it works / is that—

ASHANTI: I thought we weren't talking.

(ASHANTI dabs some of the oil on EVA's forehead.)

EVA: What are you doing?

ASHANTI: I'm anointing you, like a queen at her
coronation.

EVA: The thing is, you're really supposed to diffuse—

(ASHANTI puts a finger on EVA's lips.)

ASHANTI: Shhhh…

EVA: *(Mumbling around* ASHANTI'*s finger)* I mean, it's really expensive, even though it's artificial, so…

(ASHANTI *removes her finger and puts the essential oil bottle back, deflated.)*

ASHANTI: Sorry.

EVA: I mean, I don't…

ASHANTI: No, it's fine. Sorry. You're right.

(An awkward pause)

EVA: The diffuser's right over here, if you want to…if, you know, you want to…I don't know…

(JANE *rolls her eyes, then loudly opens and closes the basement door.)*

JANE: Eva, Mom says dinner's almost ready.

(ASHANTI *gets up and starts putting on her protective gear.)*

EVA: Isn't it basically breakfast at this point?

JANE: Mom wants to call it dinner, so please don't pick a fight with her about this.

EVA: Fine. I'll be up for dinner in a minute.

ASHANTI: I should really get going anyhow. *(She gets up and starts putting on her protective gear.)*

EVA: We still have like ten minutes until the siren goes off.

ASHANTI: I know.

EVA: Okay.…

(ASHANTI *is about to put on her protective mask, then pauses.* EVA *looks at her, expectantly.)*

ASHANTI: I changed my mind.

EVA: Um…about what?

ASHANTI: Maybe silence isn't always powerful. Sometimes the not so easy stuff is actually the most important stuff to talk about.

EVA: I...I don't understand.

(ASHANTI *smiles.*)

ASHANTI: Bye, Eva.

EVA: Bye...

(ASHANTI *puts on her mask and leaves.*)

JANE: Tragic. Just tragic.

EVA: How long were you watching?

JANE: Long enough to know that I had to put you out of your misery. Holy shit.

EVA: Thanks. Really. You're sweet.

JANE: I mean, I'd give you some pointers, but my God—you're supposed to diffuse it? Are / you even—

EVA: I am such a fuck-up, ugh!

JANE: Points for self-awareness, at least.

EVA: Can we...can we breathe together? Please?

(JANE *nods.*)

JANE: Your feet are on the ground.

EVA: My feet are on the ground.

JANE: Your body's in this space.

EVA: My body's in this space.

JANE: Put your focus on an object. Listen to my voice. Breathe in, and out. In, and out. In, and out.

(*A moment, as* EVA *and* JANE *look at each other.*)

EVA: I just don't know what to do. Pretty much ever.

JANE: Are you into Ashanti?

EVA: Yes, alright? Yes.

JANE: Then just try doing…less.

EVA: It's not that simple. You're cool, Jane. Cool people can afford to do less. Me? I have to do more just to make up for whatever core thing about me it is that turns people off.

JANE: Hey. Hey, that's not true. So you're a bit of a nerd. So you're a little…intense, sometimes. That's what makes you special. That's what makes you, well, you. Am I right, or am I right?

EVA: Possibly, I guess.

JANE: So stop fighting it. Stop trying to figure out what other people want you to say and be. That's what puts you in your head and makes you act all weird and awkward sometimes. Just say fuck it and be your intense, nerd self. Maybe that's not going to make everyone like you. But it'll make enough people love you. Like me. And Mom. And who knows? Maybe even Ash.

EVA: Really? You think?

JANE: Only one way to find out.

EVA: Maybe you're right. *(Beat)* Thanks.

JANE: Now come on. Get this stuff picked up. From the smell of things, you've got a few minutes before Mom tosses whatever she just incinerated and makes another go of it.

EVA: Yeah. Okay. Um, thanks.

(JANE *salutes and goes back upstairs.* EVA *begins gathering up the contents of the altar in her hands. She turns to put them back on the table—when she does, she suddenly sees the shadow of the antlered figure and freezes. A moment, then an echoey, slightly unworldly male voice [*CERNUNNOS*] fills the room.)*

CERNUNNOS: State thy purpose.

EVA: Oh holy shit. Holy shit holy shit holy shit…

CERNUNNOS: State thy purpose.

EVA: Imogen? Imogen, if that's you, this really isn't—

(The lights flicker, then the candles on the yoga mat suddenly light themselves.)

CERNUNNOS: STATE THY— *(He begins coughing and sputtering.)*

EVA: Oh. Oh. Are you…are you okay?

(CERNUNNOS coughs a little more.)

CERNUNNOS: The air… *(Coughs)* heavy… *(Coughs)* burning… *(Coughs)* befouled…

EVA: Yeah, we'll get to that. It's a whole thing. But you're…you're a spirit? A…deity? A…something like that?

CERNUNNOS: I am Cernunnos!

EVA: Cernunnos. Wow. I can't believe it really worked…

CERNUNNOS: Dost thou dare doubt me?!

(The ground rumbles and the flames of the candles rise up, menacingly.)

EVA: No. God no. I mean…Cernunnos no. I mean… sorry. Are you a good spirit? Please don't tell me I summoned the kind of god that eats eyeballs or souls or something like that. I mean, no offense if you do eat eyeballs. *(Pause)* DO you eat eyeballs?

CERNUNNOS: I am The Horned One! Master of beasts and all things wild! Sacred mediator between earth and mankind!

EVA: "Sacred mediator between earth and mankind"? Oh man, that's perfect.

CERNUNNOS: I— *(He breaks into another coughing fit.)*

EVA: Okay, easy, you might not want to breathe too deep. Wait. Do you even have lungs? I don't...

CERNUNNOS: Everything...feels wrong...

EVA: Do you really not know what's been going on for the last few decades?

CERNUNNOS: I hath slumbered for many ages of man. I woke not for war nor famine nor flood.

EVA: But you woke for...me? For my ritual? Really? In your face, Imogen! Ha!

CERNUNNOS: The ritual? I've seen better. But it was the power of the crystal sex magic / that—

EVA: Wait, crystal what magic now?

CERNUNNOS: Not five minutes ago! You and your consort conjured crystal sex magic at the altar!

EVA: Consort? I mean, nothing happened or anything. Really.

CERNUNNOS: The energy was most powerful.

EVA: Okay, but are we talking like a mutual, she wanted me and I wanted her equally, energy flowing back and forth sort of—

CERNUNNOS: SILENCE!

EVA: Sorry.

CERNUNNOS: The magic of the ritual, though, was strange. Diluted. Just look at me! I'm a shadow of myself. Quite literally. Tell me, which master didst thou study with?

EVA: Master? Oh. Um. I sort of just used this...

(EVA *holds up the Dark Arts for Beginners book.*)

EVA: It was my grandmother's. Back when she was going through something she says they called a "goth phase" back then. I found it in the basement like, the day after the nocturnal regulations were extended. It felt like serendipity.

CERNUNNOS: The Dark Arts for Beginners…?

EVA: Yeah. Is that bad? Have I…offended thee / or—

CERNUNNOS: Thou tryest my patience. I demand that thou explain this current state of things. The air is thick and hot. Fires burn everywhere. The seas swell. Life itself withers. What curse has befallen existence? What evil spirit has been cast upon all mortal beings?

EVA: Okay. So, um, there's this thing called climate change. Meaning humans, we…well, we fucked it all up. And the earth is turning into an uninhabitable wasteland at a scary-fast pace. And it's officially too late. That's what the scientists on the CRAD screen say.

CERNUNNOS: The coven shall perform a ritual! Thou must be skyclad at dawn, and / then take—

EVA: Oh. Hm. Yeah. Skyclad, that's, like, naked right?

CERNUNNOS: Of course!

EVA: So yeah, the air is pretty much literally poison now. Or the U V levels. We've haven't been allowed to go out without full protective gear for…what, five years now? I mean, it's the law. And dawn…that's a no-go too. It used to be we could only go out in the day when the U V levels were below code yellow. But then like every day was a code yellow or worse for something like six months, and we kind of…never went back, I guess.

(Pause)

CERNUNNOS: So no skyclad chanting at the rising sun?

EVA: No, that's pretty much part of the before time. Lots of things are.

CERNUNNOS: Well…then thou must gather at midnight where the ocean meets the shore, and wade skyclad into the waves / and—

EVA: Okay, I'm going to stop you right there. Beaches are sort of…I guess you would call them a churning hellscape these days?

CERNUNNOS: No….

EVA: Yeah, tell me about it.

CERNUNNOS: If you knew the poetry of the waves dancing among the sand, you would weep at the loss.

EVA: I do remember. At least a little. Everything went to shit when I was super young, but my grandmother lived in Florida and…I don't know. Maybe I had those memories in my head when I was trying to do the ritual.

CERNUNNOS: What memories? Tell.

EVA: I was five the last time we went, so it's only little flashes. Bits and pieces. I remember…walking on the beach and picking up a starfish. And hell, starfish are extinct now. Florida is pretty much extinct too. But I remember it all. The wet sand. That weird, rough, space alien body. That gentle sound of the waves coming in and out, in and out. The smell of the salt. The feeling of the breeze. And sometimes I'm glad that I got to experience those things, at least once. I got to make those memories. But sometimes I wish I hadn't, you know? Because every time I remember them, I think about how I won't ever feel or smell or touch anything like that ever again. Nobody will.

(A pause. The sound of sniffling)

CERNUNNOS: I feel…

EVA: Oh. Oh, are you…?

(CERNUNNOS is, in fact, crying.)

CERNUNNOS: Pain. Ache. Heaviness and lightness in all the wrong places. Like I long to take a mighty shit, but have been stopped up by a cork! It's too much to bear. Too much. (*He cries some more.*)

EVA: So that means you're going to help us, right?

CERNUNNOS: Why? Why should I help humanity? You've ruined all the gifts I've bestowed upon you.

EVA: What? No. Hell no. Absolutely not. I…I took all that time to write the ritual. And managed to pull it off. Sort of. And did the crystal thing with the vibrations. I did all that. Me. So do not play games with me. We're doing this, pal.

CERNUNNOS: How dare thou speakest to the mighty Cernunnos that way?

EVA: I dare because I have nothing to lose. Nothing. I have no future. None of us do. Come on, you're such a big deal mighty god? Fucking prove it.

(*Pause*)

CERNUNNOS: Bid the coven return.

EVA: Oh. Well. Imogen pretty much isn't speaking to me right now, and Claire just does / whatever—

CERNUNNOS: Do not doubt. Do not question. In order to put things right, I must be fully manifest.

EVA: Oh wow. Oh my God…I mean oh my Cernunnos. You'll do it? You'll fix things? You'll fix all of it? You'll save the planet? Really?

CERNUNNOS: I will. I must. First, though, the magic must be done right.

EVA: Show me. I want to know everything.

(EVA *stands by the altar and looks toward* CERNUNNOS' *shadow as lights fade.*)

Scene 3

(EVA, ASHANTI, JANE, IMOGEN, *and* CLAIRE *all stand in a semi-circle, staring up at the horned shadow that is* CERNUNNOS.)

ASHANTI: It's beautiful.

CLAIRE: It's so messed up.

IMOGEN: It's a fucking shadow.

EVA: And that shadow is going to help us. Ladies, here it is, as promised. Proof that our ritual worked.

IMOGEN: I repeat, it's a fucking shadow. Jane, you swore on your father's grave that this would be worth my time. Not really seeing the payoff here yet.

ASHANTI: You need to open your mind.

IMOGEN: Oh please. You're only into this because you want Eva to open her legs.

EVA: Really, you think she…? I mean—uh—guys, hello, we successfully summoned an ancient pagan deity. We did that. It's kind of a big deal.

ASHANTI: I'm trying to embrace this moment, Eva, but Imogen's lousy attitude is making it really hard.

IMOGEN: Oh please. What moment? It's just some lousy VR projection. And not even a really convincing one. I mean, look at those lame antlers.

CERNUNNOS: HOW DAREST THOU INSULT THE GREAT CERNUNNOS!

(CLAIRE *screams.* IMOGEN *rolls her eyes.*)

CLAIRE: The shadow thing talks! You didn't tell us it talks, Eva. Oh man, I think I feel a panic attack coming on…

ASHANTI: Claire, it's okay. This is a beautiful moment. I can hear the soul of the planet itself in that voice.

IMOGEN: Or, Eva is screwing with us and it's just a VR.

CLAIRE: Okay, you're right. You're right. It's just a VR…it's just a VR….it's Just a VR…

JANE: I dunno. I've never really heard a projection with that kind of sound capability before.

EVA: See, listen to Jane. She's a total prodigy with tech. So if she says it's not VR…

JANE: Plus, Eva is way too much of a dumbass with tech to pull off something even half as slick as this.

EVA: Okay, rude. But true.

IMOGEN: Really, Jane? You of all people are buying into this bullshit?

CERNUNNOS: The great Cernunnos is not bullshit!

IMOGEN: Whatever.

CLAIRE: Imogen, I don't know. Maybe don't make it mad. Just in case.

IMOGEN: What have I told you about being strong? Whatever this shit is, it isn't strong.

CLAIRE: I know, I know, I'm…trying.

EVA: Claire, I really appreciate your open-mindedness here. I happen to think you're being very strong, and / I just—

CLAIRE: So how do we get rid of it?

EVA: Get rid of it? No / we—

CERNUNNOS: Trickery! Treachery!

EVA: Cernunnos, uh—sir, no, she's / doesn't know what—

CLAIRE: I'm dead serious. I keep trying to tell you, we are messing with some scary stuff here. We have to put an end to it.

CERNUNNOS: The member of the coven that resembles the countenance of a rodent seekest to banish me! The insolence!

CLAIRE: I'm not exactly sure what that means, but I can tell it's hurtful. Your demon's a real jerk, Eva.

CERNUNNOS: I have ways of hurting you that you couldn't even begin to imagine.

CLAIRE: Did you just—it threatened me. You all just heard that.

EVA: He's just kidding. And, uh, Cernunnos. No offense, but Imogen kind of had a point. You're just a fucking shadow right now. If you want us to materialize you, maybe let me handle things from here.

(Beat)

CERNUNNOS: Very well…

CLAIRE: Hang on. Materialize him? May I remind you that he threatened me with bodily harm?

EVA: That's just…the way he talks. Don't take it so seriously. And it's the only way. We do a ritual, give him a physical form, then he goes out there and saves the planet. It's easy.

CLAIRE: Ritual? No. No way. No freakin' way.

IMOGEN: Seconded. The trainwreck value here is officially played out.

JANE: I think you're losing control of the room, sis.

EVA: Uh…I guess the thing is…or I guess my point is… why not?

IMOGEN: That's it? Just "why not"?

EVA: Well yeah. Why not give me a chance?

JANE: You're going to have to do better than that. (Beat) Come on, you've got this.

(EVA *thinks for a moment.*)

EVA: Okay, here's the thing. Just…listen up, everyone. I want you to think about the stakes here. Think about the last few months. And the last few years. Our lives collectively suck, yes or no?

ASHANTI: (*Softly*) My life doesn't suck when I'm with you.

EVA: It sucks less, or I hope it sucks less, but suckage is pretty relative at this point.

CLAIRE: It's kind of hard to argue with that.

IMOGEN: Are you seriously encouraging her?

CLAIRE: It's just…maybe, lately—life is kind of tipping over into the negative end of relative suckage for me. I'm not saying she's right about anything, I'm just saying…I sorta get where she's coming from. At least a little. Sorry.

IMOGEN: Okay, so life is hard? Then just be harder and get the fuck on with it already.

CLAIRE: Imogen—stop. Don't be like this.

IMOGEN: Me? You stop being like this.

CLAIRE: I'm not being like anything. I'm just—dealing, I guess.

IMOGEN: But you aren't dealing. You're whining. And if I'm the only person in your entire life who cares about you enough to say that you need to toughen up already before the collective world eats you for breakfast, then fine—bring it.

CLAIRE: I just…. I just…

IMOGEN: Spit it out. Jeez.

CLAIRE: Nevermind…

(*Weird silence*)

JANE: Okay let's just...focus here. Put everything else to the side for now and really think about what Eva's saying. We can't do anything our parents did when they were our age. No riding bikes to the park. No spending summer break at the beach. You're going to have to wear full protective gear for all of prom, which kind of defeats the point. So isn't Eva, kind of...right?

ASHANTI: Relatively speaking...I guess.

EVA: Sure! And what about the future? Think that's going to suck any less? You think things are going to get any better from here?

(They consider this.)

JANE: Mom has these old TikToks from college, right? Goofing off on the quad with Dad. Lots of ivy on the buildings around them. Someone's throwing a frisbee. You know what I'm talking about, Eva?

EVA: Obviously. She goes through all of them every year on the anniversary of the day he died. Kinda morbid if you ask me.

JANE: I mean yeah, it's lame—but that quad. I dunno. It sticks with me every time. I know I'm supposed to be sad about Dad, and I am I guess, but I'm more sad that we'll never have that.

(Everyone's quiet for a moment.)

EVA: Remember what you wanted to be when you grew up back when you were like five, Imogen? Back when we all really, really believed we could grow up to be something?

IMOGEN: *(Quietly)* A fashion designer...

EVA: Yeah, well unless you want to try to make a career out of printing paisley on protective gear or something, I'm sorry but you're kinda screwed. Claire?

CLAIRE: I…I wanted to study the whales out on Cape Cod, like my grandmother did.…

EVA: Oh jeez. Wow. Well that was kind of done, even back then, but it's really, really over now. Hell, Cape Cod pretty much doesn't even exist anymore.

ASHANTI: I wanted to be a teacher…

EVA: And the government is telling everyone they shouldn't even have kids anymore— "conservation of resources". But really, it's more like—what kind of sick asshole would choose to bring a life into a dying world? So how much of a market do you think there's going to be for teaching?

(Pause)

CLAIRE: You're right about all that. Clearly. Obviously. But…that doesn't mean any of this is even remotely a good idea.

EVA: Cernunnos says he wants to help us. And I believe him. But okay, fine—say he's lying. Say we fully materialize him, and he, I don't know, kills us all…

CERNUNNOS: I could! I could gut every last one of you! I could flay you limb by limb! Do not doubt the power of the great Cernunnos!

EVA: Okay, you are NOT helping. But say he does flay us all limb by limb or whatever. How much worse off would we really be? Doesn't it make sense to at least try…something?

JANE: But try…what exactly? Do you even have a plan here?

EVA: Of course I have a plan! Or, Cernunnos does. We do two more rituals. One to materialize him, and another to free his energy from the magic circle.

IMOGEN: Correct me if I'm wrong here, but isn't the magic circle just your mom's basement?

EVA: Same difference.

JANE: And then?

EVA: Then he goes out, heals the planet, and boom, climate change is over. Everything is clean and pure and safe again. The fires out west finally stop. We all just get to…live.

ASHANTI: It's that simple?

CERNUNNOS: Once I am manifest and free to roam, my powers are almost limitless.

EVA: Who's in?

(They all look at each other.)

ASHANTI: This is the absolute definition of my code for life. Creation instead of destruction. Healing instead of harm. Of course I'm in.

EVA: Thanks. That means a lot. I…I can't imagine doing this without you.

IMOGEN: I could puke on both of you.

JANE: You're with us—right, Imogen?

EVA: Us? So that means—you're in, Jane?

JANE: I mean, what do we have to lose? *(Beat)* Imogen?

IMOGEN: Hey, Mr. Horny. Answer me something. You can really stop the California fires? Like, don't screw with me. You swear?

CERNUNNOS: As easily as snuffing out a candle.

IMOGEN: Then yeah, sure whatever. It's not like I have anything better to do.

JANE: Claire?

IMOGEN: We're both in.

CLAIRE: Hang on. I want to hear him promise first.

EVA: Who?

CLAIRE: The horn demon thing. I want you to promise not to flay me limb by limb.

CERNUNNOS: I promise nothing.

CLAIRE: Then no. No way.

EVA: Cernnunos. Your horned majesty. Mighty one. Please. Do you want to become manifest or not?

CERNUNNOS: I do.

EVA: And did you or did you not tell me that we need the entire coven for the ritual?

CERNUNNOS: All who summoned me must participate!

EVA: Then come on…

CERNUNNOS: Oh alright. I promise not to flay *all* of your limbs.

CLAIRE: Eva!

EVA: No limb-flaying at all. None.

CERNUNNOS: None at all?

CLAIRE: No!

CERNUNNOS: But I…I…

EVA: Say it. I…

CERNUNNOS: I…

EVA: Promise…

CERNUNNOS: Promise…

EVA: Not to flay any of your limbs.

CERNUNNOS: Not to flay any of your limbs…yet.

CLAIRE: Hey!

EVA: He was kidding.

ASHANTI: I have a question.

CERNUNNOS: The one who conjured the sex magic with the high priestess! She may speak.

IMOGEN: Sex what now? I knew it. I knew it!

EVA: It's not what it sounds like. It was just…crystals and vibrations and—

IMOGEN: Vibrations. Uh-huh.

EVA: Not that kind / of—

ASHANTI: No. Eva. You don't have to act embarrassed. We experienced something with the Ice of Eternity. It's all creation and healing, right?

EVA: Even, um…crystal sex magic?

ASHANTI: Especially crystal sex magic.

JANE: Oh god, please stop saying "crystal sex magic"….

IMOGEN: Wait. I was just messing with you, but does this mean that you two are…you know?

EVA: Um. I don't—I….

(ASHANTI *takes* EVA's *hand and smiles.*)

ASHANTI: I think maybe…we are. If Eva's okay with that.

EVA: I think maybe…I am. I'm very okay with that.

CLAIRE: Aw! You guys!

CERNUNNOS: We must remain focused! The consort of the high priestess sought to ask a question.

ASHANTI: Me? Oh, um. How exactly do we conjure you? Should I go get my drum?

EVA: Okay, so don't freak out, but technically, to fully manifest a god you have to get into a little, you know…

IMOGEN: No, we don't know. What?

EVA: Um, human sacrifice.

CLAIRE: WHAT?

IMOGEN: I nominate Ashanti. It was her sluttiness that got us into this mess in the first place.

ASHANTI: But Eva, what about the code? I don't understand.

EVA: Hang on! Hang on! I said don't freak out.

CLAIRE: This is why I insisted on the no-flaying pledge!

EVA: *(To* CERNUNNOS*)* See, I told you the whole human sacrifice thing was firmly off the table.

CERNUNNOS: Humanity has grown soft and weak. Pity.

*(*EVA *takes a stuffed bull out from under the altar.)*

ASHANTI: What is it?

EVA: An effigy.

JANE: Is that…my Ferdinand?

EVA: Possibly…

JANE: You are such a little shit sometimes.

EVA: What? You didn't even notice he was gone.

ASHANTI: Tell us what we have to do.

EVA: First, we cast the circle.

JANE: *(Sighs)* I'll get Mom's butter knife.

EVA: Not…quite like that.

(Everyone else looks on, puzzled, as EVA *takes a bottle out from under the altar. It's filled with a mysterious liquid. She opens it and begins trickling the liquid onto the ground in a rough circle around the group.)*

JANE: Oh man. Eva…

*(*IMOGEN *covers her nose.)*

IMOGEN: That is disgusting.

JANE: Please tell me you did not piss in that bottle.

EVA: It was that or the menstrual blood of a virgin.

CERNUNNOS: An inferior and disappointing substitute!

(EVA *shrugs as she finishes.*)

EVA: And now, the effigy.

CERNUNNOS: Cannot we at least procure a real bull?

EVA: I told you, just about all large mammals are extinct or about to be. The only bulls left are in underground sanctuaries.

CERNUNNOS: Very well. Then this will have to suffice.

EVA: We have to make it as alive as possible, then we… sacrifice it. Now repeat after me. I offer up the life force of my own body.

(*Pause*)

CLAIRE: Metaphorically, right?

EVA: Sure. Metaphorically. Now say it. I offer up the life force of my own body.

ALL: I offer up the life force of my own body.

EVA: I offer up this sacrifice to the great Cernunnos.

ALL: I offer up this sacrifice to the great Cernunnos.

EVA: So that he may cleanse us all.

ALL: So that he may cleanse us all.

EVA: DRINK, YE GODS!

ALL: DRINK, YE GODS!

(EVA *takes a serrated knife from under the altar, slices her own palm and lets the blood trickle on to the effigy.*)

IMOGEN: Woah.

JANE: Hardcore.

CLAIRE: You said that whole life force of the body thing was a metaphor!

EVA: Yeah, well I lied. Now who's first?

(ASHANTI *picks up the knife.*)

ASHANTI: I'm fully committed to walking this path with you. (*She slices her palm and trickles the blood over the effigy.*)

EVA: Now repeat after me—I bestow life that thou may sacrifice it.

ASHANTI: I bestow life that thou may sacrifice it.

EVA: Who's next?

(*Everyone's silent.*)

EVA: Jane?

JANE: Yeah, I'm renegotiating the terms of my involvement in this.

EVA: Seriously?

JANE: Seriously. What's it worth to you?

EVA: A month of meat rations?

JANE: Six months.

EVA: Six?!

JANE: That shit's going to scar. My hands are my best feature.

EVA: Ugh, fine, six months of meat rations. Done.

(JANE *slices her palm and trickles the blood over the effigy.*)

EVA: Now repeat—

JANE: Yeah yeah yeah, I got it. I bestow life that thou may sacrifice it.

CERNUNNOS: Yes. Yes. Do you not feel the throb of life growing?

IMOGEN: Okay, creepy much?

JANE: Come on, Imogen, you're up.

IMOGEN: Oh no. Hell no. I faint at the sight of blood.

ASHANTI: This from the girl who pierced her own nipples with a safety pin and a lighter.

IMOGEN: Wait, how did you...

(ASHANTI *looks at* CLAIRE, *who looks down at her shoes.*)

IMOGEN: Oh fuck you and your big fucking mouth.

(IMOGEN *picks up the knife, marches over to* CLAIRE, *and grabs her wrist.*)

CLAIRE: Hey!

IMOGEN: Claire wants to go next.

(IMOGEN *slices* CLAIRE's *palm and roughly rubs it over the effigy.*)

IMOGEN: She bestows her gossipy, disloyal life that thou may sacrifice it, even though it's stupid and a terrible friend—right, Claire?

CLAIRE: Right....

EVA: She has to actually say it.

CLAIRE: Ugh. I bestow life that thou may sacrifice it.

EVA: Imogen, now—

IMOGEN: Alright, alright. Fine.

(IMOGEN *draws the knife across her palm and trickles the blood over the effigy.*)

IMOGEN: I bestow life that thou may sacrifice it or whatever.

(*There's a hum in the air now. A glow. Everyone looks at each other, uneasy.*)

EVA: Arise, child of blood.

ALL: Arise, child of blood.

CERNUNNOS: Yes. Yes. It is working....

EVA: Be born to die.

ALL: Be born to die.

EVA: So that all may live again.

ALL: So that all may live again.

(The hum and the glow increase. EVA takes a book of matches out from under the altar and lights a match.)

EVA: Ignite, and be abundant.

ALL: Ignite, and be abundant.

(EVA touches the match to the effigy, which ignites.)

CLAIRE: Is that—safe?

(As the effigy burns, a sudden, semi-human, unearthly screaming can be heard.)

CERNUNNOS: LET THE FIRE CLEANSE

EVA: LET THE FIRE CLEANSE

ALL: LET THE FIRE CLEANSE

(The screaming gets louder. EVA collapses to the floor.)

ASHANTI: Eva!

(As ASHANTI moves towards EVA, there's a crack and a blinding flash of light. As the light slowly returns to normal, we see JANE putting the effigy out with a small fire extinguisher. ASHANTI is holding EVA, who is unconscious. Where the shadow of CERNUNNOS once was, there is a man, in his mid-to-late 30s, dressed casually in jeans and a T-shirt.)

IMOGEN: What the…?

CLAIRE: Who are you?

MAN/CERNUNNOS: You know who I am.

(As JANE turns around, her mouth falls open. She drops the fire extinguisher with a clatter.)

JANE: Eva…

ASHANTI: I think she's coming to. Eva….Eva, are you alright?

EVA: Ash…

JANE: What did you do, Eva?

EVA: I…I…

(EVA *sits up as she opens her eyes. She looks up at*
ASHANTI, *smiles, then looks over at the man and scrambles*
to her feet. She looks at the man, then at JANE, *then back at*
the man again.)

EVA: Dad…?

DAD/CERNUNNOS: Hey, Bucky. I've missed you.

IMOGEN: Bucky?!?!

JANE: That was, uh, Dad's nickname for her. I…shit…

DAD/CERNUNNOS: Hey Satch. I've missed ya, pal.

JANE: Oh no. No no no no.

CLAIRE: So wait. Does this mean Eva and Jane are…
demon spawn?

IMOGEN: Apparently.

ASHANTI: I think there are forces at work we don't
understand, so we shouldn't be so quick to label any of
this. Right Eva?

(No response)

ASHANTI: Uh, right Jane?

JANE: This is…this is just…fuck, dude…

DAD/CERNUNNOS: I know it's a lot. It's kind of a lot for
me, too. And I remember how anxious you could get.

JANE: The last time we saw each other you had just
spent two years dying. Plus I was thirteen. Anxious
kind of comes with the territory of being thirteen.

EVA: But where did Cernunnos go? And how…how
did you come back?

DAD/CERNUNNOS: Hey, don't worry about that stuff right now. How about we just spend a little time together, huh?

IMOGEN: And I'm out.

ASHANTI: Imogen, don't.

IMOGEN: Nope, this is way too creepy for me. I'm done. Come on, Claire.

ASHANTI: Claire…

CLAIRE: Two words Ash: Demon. Spawn.

(IMOGEN and CLAIRE get up and start putting their protective gear back on.)

EVA: We're not…we're not…I mean that's not…that's Dad. It's just Dad. Right Jane?

JANE: Why are you asking me? It was your stupid ritual.

DAD/CERNUNNOS: I'm gonna need you to sit back down, girls.

IMOGEN: I don't know if you're Cernunnos or Eva's dad or whatever, but I do know that you're not *my* dad, so you know what? Bite me.

DAD/CERNUNNOS: I SAID SIT DOWN.

CLAIRE: I…I think we should do what he says.

(IMOGEN and CLAIRE slowly put their gear down and return to the group.)

DAD/CERNUNNOS: Thanks, girls. Nobody's going to ruin this for my Eva. Just so we're clear on that.

EVA: But…what exactly is "this", Dad? What's going on?

DAD/CERNUNNOS: Well isn't that a silly question. Don't we have a mission to complete?

EVA: Like, a secret spy mission?

DAD/CERNUNNOS: Yeah, exactly. With sunglasses and special disguises and everything.

EVA: What's the mission?

ASHANTI: Eva? You're not making any sense. I'm trying to keep my heart open to this whole experience, but the weird vibes here are really starting to kill my spiritual high.

IMOGEN: Let the record show that Ash of all people said this is too weird for her—*Ash*.

JANE: No, it's uh…CIA Agent. It's a game Dad made up. It's…

IMOGEN: Really fucking creepy and weird.

JANE: Yeah. That.

DAD/CERNUNNOS: C'mon Satch, you're happy to see me, aren't you?

JANE: Even if you were actually my father—which, to be clear, I don't believe for one fucking second—why would I be happy to see you?

EVA: Don't worry about her, Dad. She's just being a brat. She was older but I was the mature one. You always said so. Remember?

JANE: Don't, Eva. Please. He was always…pitting us against each other. Talking shit about us to each other. You were just the favorite because you took the bait.

EVA: For once in our lives, somebody loved me more than they loved you, and you just couldn't take it.

JANE: Well guess what? He left you just the same as he left me.

EVA: What do you mean left? He had cancer.

JANE: Because he was too much of a smug, arrogant prick to wear his gear out.

EVA: Don't talk about Dad that way! Don't!

JANE: "Screw that, Satch. I'm not gonna let the goverment tell me what to do. I wanna feel the sun on my face." Remember that, [air quotes] "Dad"?

DAD/CERNUNNOS: I can't change the past. I wish I could.

JANE: "I'd rather live forty-five minutes truly free than forty-five years in fear." How about that little gem of wisdom?

EVA: Stop, Jane! Just stop! Dad, I want to play CIA Agent. I do. What's the mission?

DAD/CERNUNNOS: We'll need everyone to play.

(Pause)

EVA: Well come on, everyone. What's the problem?

IMOGEN: I mean, this is just a guess, but it could be the teeny tiny fact that until about five minutes ago there was a horned shadow demon thing standing right where your dead Dad is now. Doesn't that seem a little weird to you?

EVA: Not really.

ASHANTI: I want to say, Eva, that if you and Jane are descended from some sort of magical being, I would never discriminate. I'd celebrate it. And I'd never use a derogatory term like "demon spawn". I think people of all backgrounds are beautiful. But I do think it's worth finding out for sure. Don't you?

EVA: Oh, I know exactly what's going on here.

CLAIRE: You do?

EVA: What? Don't sound so weirded out about it. We just got the ritual wrong. I mean, I absolutely did not know what I was doing, right? That's pretty clear. I messed it up the first day, and I messed it up again here. Instead of conjuring up Cernunnos, we brought my dad back from the dead.

CLAIRE: That's pretty insane.

EVA: And everything else about this is so normal? Why can't any of you just believe that something good could happen to me?

ASHANTI: But even if all this is true…we have a mission here, Eva. We're supposed to be healing Mother Earth. Shouldn't we try to get back on track?

EVA: No. Or not today, at least. I don't care about Mother Earth right now. I care about my dad, Ash. He's here—he's actually here—and the only thing I want to do is play CIA Agent with him. I feel like that's not too much to ask for. Can we, Dad? Can we play now?

DAD/CERNUNNOS: I told you, Bucky. We'll need everyone. The whole group.

EVA: What do we have to do?

DAD/CERNUNNOS: First, we all have to hold hands.

(*Everyone looks at each other doubtfully.*)

EVA: What? Come on. CIA Agent is so much fun. It was always our favorite. Right Jane?

JANE: I don't know. That was your thing with Dad, not mine.

EVA: Well it was my favorite. It was. You're all going to love it.

IMOGEN: So that's going to be a hard no for me. This is either a super rapey situation or a mass murder situation, or both, but either way, I'm not so into it.

EVA: He's not asking for anything weird / just to—

IMOGEN: I get it. I do. Me of all people, right?

EVA: Just because your dad's dead too doesn't mean you get anything. Lots of people's parents are dead.

In case you haven't noticed, it's kind of a thing these days.

IMOGEN: Ugh. Okay. I can't believe I'm fucking saying this, but remember what Mr Mike said about fantasies?

CLAIRE: Mr Mike?

IMOGEN: I moved here from Cali like the week Eva's dad died, and they stuck both of us with the same grief counselor. Mr Mike. Being allowed to use his first name was supposed to trick us into feeling comfortable with him or whatever. Remember that asshole?

EVA: He was always trying to give me half-melted hard candy. And he smelled like the basement of a thrift store.

IMOGEN: That candy pissed me off. Like, sorry your dad literally died in a fire—have a Werther's. But Mr Mike did say one cool thing, I thought. Remember that thing he said about dream life versus real life?

EVA: Imogen, this isn't…

IMOGEN: It's nice to have a dream life where everything's perfect and happy, but it's still really important to eventually come back to your real life and work on making that as happy as you can. That always stuck with me. Remember?

(EVA *considers this.*)

EVA: Oh my God. Imogen. If we brought back my Dad, maybe we / can—

IMOGEN: Nope. Nope nope nope nope…

EVA: Maybe we can bring back your dad too.

IMOGEN: I've attempted to do my good deed for the year. Someone else want to step in here.

JANE: Alright, alright. Dad.

DAD/CERNUNNOS: Hey sweetie. What's up?

JANE: What the hell are you?

DAD/CERNUNNOS: I don't know what you're talking about, Satch. I'm your dad.

JANE: Nuh-uh. Whatever kind of shenanigans you're gunning for here, clearly the group is not on board, so you're going to have to come clean.

DAD/CERNUNNOS: I really don't get why you're all being like this. You're the ones who invited me.

EVA: Wait. Invited you. What are you saying?

DAD/CERNUNNOS: I guess I'm sort of, kind of, maybe… Cernunnos. But only sort of!

CLAIRE: Then Eva and Jane aren't demon spawn. Just to clarify.

DAD/CERNUNNOS: I have all of their father's memories. His feelings. His essence. But he was human, and so are they.

EVA: Then you lied. You…why'd you have to ask that, Jane? Why'd you have to ruin it?

JANE: How is this my fault?

DAD/CERNUNNOS: My true form would literally sear your eyeballs into puddles of goo. I had to choose something. I was planning to manifest as Alistair Crowley, but then I inhaled the smoke of your blood. Yours, Eva, and yours, Jane. One bloodline combining. It was so powerful. I rode that blood-smoke back to your father's essence. I thought that would be nice. Easier for you. If you'd rather, I can re-manifest as Alistair. But I'm warning you, he has a bit of a sadistic streak. And if you're worried about somebody being rapey, well…

EVA: Wait. You have his…essence?

DAD/CERNUNNOS: All that he was courses through me.

EVA: Then stay. I want my dad to stay.

ASHANTI: Are you sure that's...healthy?

EVA: I don't care.

JANE: He was my father too. What about what I want?

EVA: I was closer to him. This is a way bigger thing to me than it is to you.

JANE: No. No! That is...so, so unfair.

EVA: How is it unfair? You barely even care that he died in the first place.

JANE: Just because I have complicated feelings about Dad doesn't mean that I don't have feelings at all. It doesn't mean that I don't care. Or that I don't miss him. Or that it doesn't feel really weird and upsetting and freaky that he's here. But I guess that doesn't matter. My feelings about Dad haven't ever mattered. Not compared to yours, at least. You always took up all the space. You sucked up all the air in the room. Even after Dad was gone, people still could not let me forget how much you were his favorite. "Take care of your little sister, Jane. You know how close she and your dad were" "Jane, go check on Eva. She's taking this so hard." Oh, Eva's sad again. Fix it, Jane. Eva won't come out of her room again? Talk to her, Jane. Drop everything to make sure she's OK, every time.

DAD/CERNUNNOS: I'm sorry, Jane. I'm sorry.

JANE: Don't do that. You're not him.

EVA: But...he is Dad. That's what he said. He is. It can't hurt to at least, you know, listen to what he has to say.

(Pause)

JANE: Why?

EVA: Like I said, he says / he—

JANE: No. I'm asking him. Why did you love Eva so much more? What did I do that was so wrong?

DAD/CERNUNNOS: You did nothing wrong. Nothing. I think maybe...well, maybe you just scared me a little.

JANE: Scared you? I was just a kid.

DAD/CERNUNNOS: It's just that you weren't so... generous with your love, you could say. Eva was all about the attention and the hugs and the "I love yous". You, kiddo? You were a little harder to know. And I guess your Dad...I didn't know how to handle it. So we kept our distance a little. I'm not saying it was right. But people are...flawed, really.

(JANE *considers what was just said, then shakes her head, as if rejecting his words.*)

JANE: No. This is...weird. I can't. I won't. Let's just... do whatever we have to do here, and I'll be cool. But to be clear, I'm not calling that thing Dad. And it's not allowed to call me Satch anymore, got it?

DAD/CERNUNNOS: Whatever you want, Jane. But look—and this is for everyone. Listen up, please. You summoned me here for a reason, didn't you?

EVA: To save the planet from a climate catastrophe that's going to leave the surface uninhabitable within our lifetimes and will probably kill us all before we have a chance to hit middle age.

DAD/CERNUNNOS: So shouldn't we get down to business, then?

CLAIRE: Why should we trust you? You already tried to trick us once.

DAD/CERNUNNOS: I'm sorry about that. Eva and Jane's dad, he cared about all of you. He wanted you to feel safe and comfortable, so that's what I wanted too. I thought framing things a different way might help.

ASHANTI: You really want to help us, then?

DAD/CERNUNNOS: I absorbed this man's memories, so I want to take care of you. I want to help.

EVA: See, I told you. I told all of you.

DAD/CERNUNNOS: We have to do the second part of the ritual now. The one that lets me out into the world. Now come on, everyone. All we have to do is hold hands, say a few words, and that's it. The world is reborn.

IMOGEN: Does anyone else find this whole "the world is reborn" thing to be, I don't know, suspiciously vague?

EVA: What's vague about it? We just have to open the circle, call the quarters, say a few words, and boom, climate change is done and we've saved the planet. What else is there to know?

ASHANTI: Maybe we should at least make sure that we aren't doing any harm. Creation and healing, right Eva?

(EVA and ASHANTI look at each other.)

EVA: Creation and healing. Fine. Okay. (Beat) Dad?

DAD/CERNUNNOS: Yes sweetie?

EVA: Reassure them. Go on.

DAD/CERNUNNOS: We will purify the planet together. I assure you.

EVA: But I think the sticking point is kind of…well, what exactly does that involve?

DAD/CERNUNNOS: Once I'm free to roam, and my energy can mingle with the planet, I'll be able to purge it of all toxins. To literally pull the poisons out and cast them into the abyss.

EVA: Well great. That's about what we had in mind.

DAD/CERNUNNOS: Suck the greenhouse gases out of the air.

EVA: Good, good.

DAD/CERNUNNOS: Purify the oceans of trash and excess acidity.

EVA: The oceans! Hear that, Claire?

DAD/CERNUNNOS: Leech the heavy metals and poisons from the soil.

EVA: See guys, I told you that this / was all—

DAD/CERNUNNOS: Purify the very planet of its human plague.

(Silence. Everyone stares at DAD/CERNUNNOS.*)*

CLAIRE: Come again?

DAD/CERNUNNOS: The last and most important part of purification. Humanity was the cause of this curse. To kill a poison tree, one must pull it out at the root. I'll purge humankind from the planet.

JANE: So…global genocide. Cool, cool.

DAD/CERNUNNOS: For the good of the Earth. Otherwise we'll just be right back in this situation all over again in another couple hundred years. Gotta be proactive. I'm sure you kids understand.

ASHANTI: Oh my goddess…

IMOGEN: So. You were saying, Eva?

EVA: This is…Dad, you're not explaining it right. We're not talking…genocide-genocide, right?

CLAIRE: Genocide is generally an all-or-nothing proposition.

EVA: No, but…but…

DAD/CERNUNNOS: Oh. Right. Humans don't like to die. I forgot about that. Well, honesty's the best policy anyhow. And deep down, you know I'm right.

ASHANTI: No no no. This goes against…everything. Everything I believe in.

DAD/CERNUNNOS: Do you remember the way you cried the first spring that the crocuses didn't come back? It felt like your heart got stepped on. We can bring back the crocuses and the roses and all the flowers, Ashanti. We can restore everything to the way it once was.

ASHANTI: I never told Eva's dad that. I never even told Eva that. How did you…?

DAD/CERNUNNOS: Half of me is still Cernunnos. And Cernunnos knows everything. I know that you sing when nobody else is around, Imogen. Always songs from the before time. Adele and Lorde. Things your grandparents used to like. You have a beautiful voice.

IMOGEN: No I don't. Shut up. Singing's for sappy assholes.

DAD/CERNUNNOS: Jane, Morgan from down the street likes you too. They're just waiting for you to make the first move.

EVA: Morgan? Oooooh, I knew it.

JANE: That…that was private. Not cool.

DAD/CERNUNNOS: And Claire, I'm so sorry about your mother. That must be hard.

IMOGEN: Wait. What?

CLAIRE: Um.…

DAD/CERNUNNOS: I have wisdom and knowledge none of you could ever fathom. Not to be a jerk about it, but your tiny little consciousnesses just don't even have the capacity for the kind of perspective a god has.

You just have to trust me when I say that this is for the best.

CLAIRE: Okay. How do we banish it, Eva? There has to be a spell or chant or something in your book for that.

DAD/CERNUNNOS: Honestly, kids, I'm going to remind you to watch your manners. You're the ones who invited me. I'm starting to feel a little insulted here.

IMOGEN: This is all some grade-A emotionally manipulative bullshit right here.

DAD/CERNUNNOS: Watch yourself, missy. I might look like a slightly out-of-shape suburban dad, but I'm still an all-powerful demon.

IMOGEN: Is that supposed to be a threat?

(DAD/CERNUNNOS *glares at* IMOGEN, *hold his arm up in the air, and makes a fist.* IMOGEN's *eyes go wide. She clutches her chest.*)

CLAIRE: Imogen, are you okay?

IMOGEN: Whatever….you're…doing…please….stop.

DAD/CERNUNNOS: Oh. Oh, so you feel that?

(IMOGEN *nods frantically, gasping.*)

DAD/CERNUNNOS: That's me squeezing your heart. Literally. It doesn't feel nice, does it?

ASHANTI: Oh my God! Eva, do something!

EVA: Dad, please.

DAD/CERNUNNOS: Don't worry. I'm not going to squeeze any harder than this. But I could. Understand me? I could, very easily. So…a little more respect. Please.

(DAD/CERNUNNOS *releases his fist.* IMOGEN *crumples to the floor.* CLAIRE *rushes to her side.* IMOGEN *waves her off.*)

IMOGEN: I'm fine. I'm fine.

DAD/CERNUNNOS: No hard feelings, Imogen. Or anyone. I just need you to really understand the stakes here.

IMOGEN: Hey, respect, man. Mission accomplished.

ASHANTI: Respect? He's going to kill us all!

DAD/CERNUNNOS: No. Think of that as a...show of force. I still need you all to perform the ritual that frees me. If you don't, I'm stuck in this basement. You basically have an insurance policy.

CLAIRE: Sure. We free you, and THEN you kill us all.

DAD/CERNUNNOS: Alright, true, that's a fair point.

EVA: Or what about...a compromise?

ASHANTI: What is there to compromise about? You're not making any sense.

EVA: Look, Dad has a point. Humanity fucked up. Our parents and grandparents and great grandparents brought this on the planet and on all of us, and given the chance, a lot of the assholes in charge are probably just going to do it again. Because people suck. I can't argue with that.

JANE: Okay sis, that's just about enough thinking for tonight. How about we talk upstairs for a minute, huh?

EVA: No, hang on, I'm not done. Our parents and grandparents, they did this, but we, as in me and Jane and Imogen and Claire and our whole generation, this is not our fault. We didn't ask for any of this.

CLAIRE: What are you saying?

EVA: I'm saying hold the right people responsible. Screw the adults. We're better off without them. They did this to us. They literally killed the planet. Let them get what they deserve. And then let the rest of us, the innocents, let us rebuild.

DAD/CERNUNNOS: You're saying we wipe out the adults, but spare the youth?

EVA: Climate change was officially declared irreversible, what, six years ago?

CLAIRE: March 10, 2050. So, seven years as of last week.

EVA: Okay, so anyone who was still under eighteen when that happened couldn't really practically do anything about it because they were still kids, so they're off the hook. So if you're twenty-five or over, thanks for nothing, goodbye. Twenty-four and under, let's rebuild and repopulate the planet in a responsible, sustainable way. What do you say?

DAD/CERNUNNOS: No. I'm sorry, but no.

EVA: But...but...

DAD/CERNUNNOS: Human nature is simply irredeemable. Age has nothing to do with it.

EVA: Okay, but...you're my dad, right? At least kind of? On some level?

DAD/CERNUNNOS: I told you, when you and Jane added your blood / to the—

EVA: Right, right. So, do you really want to kill your kids?

DAD/CERNUNNOS: What?

EVA: Murder us. Your daughters. You wouldn't do that, would you, Daddy?

DAD/CERNUNNOS: Sometimes you, uh, have to make hard choices...

(EVA *nudges* JANE.)

EVA: Say something....

JANE: I have nothing to say to that thing. And this whole scheme of yours is insane anyhow.

EVA: Shouldn't we at least get him to not want to off us, first? Then take things from there?

JANE: Fine. Fine! Okay. Um…remember when I fell off my bike when I was six, Dad? And I had to get staples in my head and the doctor were worried about a brain hematoma or whatever? I never saw you cry so hard, ever.

DAD/CERNUNNOS: I blamed myself. I was supposed to be watching you.…

JANE: Well killing Eva and me and all our friends would be worse than that feeling. A LOT worse.

(DAD/CERNUNNOS *stares at* JANE, *then* EVA, *then* JANE *again.*)

DAD/CERNUNNOS: Damn this weak vessel…I knew I should've just manifested as Alistair Crowley.

EVA: So, do we have a deal?

DAD/CERNUNNOS: What if I just spare you and your friends?

EVA: And doom us to a miserable, lonely existence wandering around an empty planet? I thought you loved me, Daddy.…

DAD/CERNUNNOS: Alright, alright! You just have to promise, and I mean promise, that your generation will do a better job at not burning down the planet.

EVA: We've lived through the consequences. How could we not?

DAD/CERNUNNOS: Then the coven agrees to perform the unbinding ritual?

EVA: Of course. Tell Dad you're good, everyone. (*Pause*) Go on.

JANE: Maybe just…give everyone a minute to process, Eva. It's kind of a lot.

IMOGEN: Oh, I'm one hundred percent in.

CLAIRE: Imogen, seriously? That thing tried to kill you!

IMOGEN: Eh, I've had worse. And besides, everyone's finally talking a little sense around here. Fuck the old people who jacked up our shit before we got a chance to have lives. Fuck them for not giving me a chance to do recreational drugs out in Malibu or spend all of Spring Break drunk at an outdoor bar in Florida or go backpacking across Europe with a German D J whose last name I don't know but who's A-plus at oral. I don't care if it's selfish. The older generations, they were the goddamn selfish ones. Now it's my turn. So yes, I am all the way in.

EVA: Well…great. Thanks.

ASHANTI: No! No! What's wrong with you? What's wrong with all of you? Imogen, I don't expect better from you, but Eva…Eva, how can you say those things? What about the code? This is pretty much nothing but…harm and destruction. It's literally against everything I believe in!

EVA: Ash, hang on…

ASHANTI: Our parents. Imogen, Eva, you already lost your fathers. Do you want to lose your mothers, too?

IMOGEN: I mean, not to sound too cold, but sure. That bitch is so annoying.

EVA: Ash, chances are, they're going to die pretty soon anyhow. Your parents, my mom, everyone. With the cancer rates and the storms and the fires, it's not like anyone's living to 80 these days.

ASHANTI: But I just can't perpetuate harm. I…I have principles.

IMOGEN: Oh my God, you are so black and white. That's what's always been so fucking annoying about you. You're great at puking back up all these ten thousand dollars words that you sort of know the definition of, but you haven't actually lived enough life to really know what they really mean. Like, get back to me about principles ten years from now.

ASHANTI: Fine! I will!

EVA: Except…you can't Ash. Because if we do nothing, when we had a chance to do something, the world ends—that is no exaggeration. It ends pretty goddamn soon, too. You know that. And it'll be our fault for doing nothing.

ASHANTI: That's not fair. That's absolutely, positively, spiritually and ethically unfair.

CLAIRE: Will it hurt? When the people are… annihilated. Will it hurt?

EVA: I don't….Dad?

DAD/CERNUNNOS: They will be returned to the dust of the earth. Their bodies will dissolve back into the elements they were made from. It'll feel kind of nice, actually. Like a giant exhalation.

CLAIRE: I want to believe you. I really, really do.

IMOGEN: Oh my God. You know what hurts? Life. Who cares if dying hurts for the adults? It's not like they're going to be around to bitch about it.

CLAIRE: You know what, Imogen? Fuck off.

IMOGEN: EXCUSE me?

CLAIRE: Fuck. Off.

IMOGEN: I don't know what's gotten into you / but I—

CLAIRE: I've been trying to tell you what's gotten into me. For days. But you won't listen.

JANE: Wait. Is this about that thing he said about your mom….?

CLAIRE: She never listens to me. Ever. You're supposed to be my best friend, Imogen, but you treat me like shit. Pretty much always.

IMOGEN: Claire. What's going on with your mom...?

CLAIRE: Oh, now you want to know? How novel.

IMOGEN: What's that supposed to mean?

CLAIRE: Any time I try to say what I'm thinking or feeling, you tell me I'm annoying or I'm whiny or you give me shit for not saying exactly what you want me to say.

IMOGEN: Because you're going to get hurt out there, Claire. Out in the real world. You're all sweet and wide-eyed and innocent. And that fucking scares me for you. Sweet people get ripped to shreds.

CLAIRE: The only person ripping me to shreds is you. And I really needed you this week.

IMOGEN: You're right. I'm a stupid evil bitch, and I'm sorry. (Beat) What's wrong with your mom?

CLAIRE: Something...bad. I mean, you don't have to be Cernunnos to figure it out.

IMOGEN: Skin cancer, or lung cancer?

CLAIRE: Lung...

IMOGEN: Fuck.

ASHANTI: Oh no...

JANE: Claire, I'm so sorry.

CLAIRE: I thought I could...I don't know...I tried to not be dramatic about it—like you always say, Imogen. I mean, I'm not so special. Like, over half of people Mom's age are going to get it. But...I couldn't help it. My anxiety was like...woah. And I just wanted to talk to you about it, but I...I.... (She is starting to break down.)

IMOGEN: I'm breaking my rule about sappy feelings here, okay? Mark this moment.

(IMOGEN *opens her arms.* CLAIRE *walks into them.*)

(A hug)

IMOGEN: I've never forgotten the way you were there for me. When I came here and didn't know anyone and was going the fuck through it, with my dad and all that shit. You actually, like sought me out, even though I was rude and mean and sad all the time. You didn't even know me. You so didn't have to do that. I know you didn't have to do that. So…I'm going to be there for you now. The way you were there for me. Whether you like it or not.

(CLAIRE *breaks the hug.*)

CLAIRE: That sounds…good.

IMOGEN: Good. You okay?

(CLAIRE *nods.*)

EVA: This whole thing…it's not going to hurt them, Claire. You heard him. So…

CLAIRE: If it's really going to be like breathing out… then, maybe…

ASHANTI: Claire, please. I know you're very vulnerable right now, but think about this.

CLAIRE: I have, and I think maybe Eva has a point about all this. I mean, she's being disturbingly sociopathic in the totally breezy way she talks about the whole thing, but she still might be kind of…right.

ASHANTI: Mass murder is not right. It can't be.

CLAIRE: What are our options here? The quick, instant, painless death of half the population, or the slow, agonizing, excruciating death of the entire population?

ASHANTI: But it's different when we're the ones causing it.

CLAIRE: Yeah, I'm not sure if I agree there.

EVA: Jane? What about you?

JANE: So I'm just going to circle back to Claire's earlier sociopath comment, because that's kind of where my head is right now.

EVA: Come on, don't be an asshole. Not now.

JANE: I mean hell, maybe you're right and we have no choice here, but…you're talking about literally killing Mom. That doesn't bother you, even a little?

EVA: She's so upset and depressed and miserable all the time, maybe she'll be better off.

JANE: I can't believe you'd say that.

EVA: What? She spends eighty percent of her time crying. She cries when the food generator dings.

JANE: So, what? She deserves to die because she cries? Is that really what you're saying?

EVA: No…not exactly…

JANE: I love Mom. With everything I've got. The way you were with Dad, that's how I am with Mom. And if you ever paid any attention to anyone besides yourself, you'd know that.

EVA: Of course I know that. Of course. And if your feelings get to be complicated about Dad, then mine get to be complicated about Mom.

JANE: Difference is, I didn't kill Dad.

EVA: I'm going to feel sad, and guilty, and self-hating, and whatever else—I know I will. But right now, I can't slow down to think about it too much. I can't. I just have to push ahead and do what we have to do. I can live with the regret for the rest of my life if I have to, but that starts tomorrow. Today, we have a job to do.

JANE: Maybe you can find a way to not think about it right now. But I can't. That's not who I am.

IMOGEN: I dunno. The idea of repopulating the earth sounds…fun.

JANE: Are you really making this into a sex thing?

IMOGEN: What can I say? I'm a deep well of complication and moral ambiguity.

DAD/CERNUNNOS: Kids. Save the hormones for later, and focus. Please. We don't have time to screw around. My power's waning, and I need all of you. The entire coven. Or this won't work.

ASHANTI: Then I'm going to save you all a lot of time and say it loud and proud: no. Absolutely not. Not in a thousand years. I don't care if you think it's stupid or naive, Imogen, but I live my life by a code, and all of this is fundamentally against it, in every way. And if you really need us for your unbinding ritual, that means I have veto power here, and I am exercising it.

EVA: Ash, just calm down / and—

ASHANTI: Do not tell me to calm down. I thought we had something beautiful together. I thought I knew you. I thought I looked into your soul. But no. I was wrong. You're…you're not who I thought you were. And you know what? I think I'm ready to go home. Goodbye.

(ASHANTI *makes her way towards the coat rack, where her protective gear hangs.*)

EVA: Wait!

ASHANTI: I'm done talking to you. And I mean done. You and I are through, Eva.

(EVA *looks around her frantically.*)

EVA: Somebody do something....

DAD/CERNUNNOS: Technically, all we need is her body.

(*Everyone looks at* DAD/CERNUNNOS.)

DAD/CERNUNNOS: What? We're talking about wiping 5 billion people from the planet. What's one more?

JANE: Hold up. I thought the ritual was our insurance policy or whatever. But you can just kill us and use our bodies as what...batteries?

DAD/CERNUNNOS: No. Well...sort of. That's only part of it. I need at least a few of you to chant the sacred words. And the more of you do it, the more likely it is to work. But I could certainly spare at least one voice.

(ASHANTI *turns to face* EVA.)

ASHANTI: Well there you have it. Might as well just kill me now, Eva. I mean, he's right, what's one more at this point?

EVA: No, that's not...can we just talk about this? For a minute? You have to admit there's at least a little bit of gray area here.

ASHANTI: There isn't. Not to me.

EVA: Could you all just...give us a minute to talk, maybe?

JANE: I think I'm going to sit with Mom. Talk to her. Say...oh God. Say goodbye. Just in case.

EVA: Does that mean you're...

JANE: It means I'm thinking about it. That's all.

EVA: Thanks, Jane. Really.

JANE: Imogen, Claire? If you want to make holo calls to your folks, you can use my room.

IMOGEN: I'm good.

CLAIRE: (*Through clenched teeth*) Imogen...

IMOGEN: Fine, fine. But when we get back, you two better either be drawing down the quarters or whatever to take out all the old people, or fucking. Or both, if it's that kind of ritual.

JANE: And just when I thought my day couldn't get any more disturbing. Thanks for that.

IMOGEN: I live to serve.

(JANE, IMOGEN, *and* CLAIRE *exit upstairs.* DAD/ CERNUNNOS *steps back a bit, into the shadows.* EVA *and* ASHANTI *look at each other.*)

ASHANTI: If you're going to talk then talk.

EVA: Let's sit by the altar.

(EVA *takes two cushions and sets them by the altar. She sits on one, and pats the empty cushion next to her.* ASHANTI *sighs.*)

ASHANTI: Fine. But it's not going to work. Not again. I see you now. Like, really see you.

(*Reluctantly,* ASHANTI *sits down next to* EVA.)

EVA: Just take a minute and think about this. We did it. We actually did it. Aside from however you feel about what happens from here, isn't that pretty amazing? We made something impossible happen. Together. You have to at least see how beautiful and amazing that is.

ASHANTI: So what, you're saying doing something - literally anything—is beautiful and amazing? Rapists do things. Serial killers do things. Not all actions are good actions.

EVA: Do you think you know everything, Ash?

ASHANTI: That's absolutely and completely unfair

EVA: No, I'm really, truly asking. Do you?

ASHANTI: No, I don't think I know everything, but I know right from wrong.

EVA: But maybe this time you don't. Maybe you're just too close to it. This is what the ancient ones think is right. This is what the planet itself is telling us it needs. And maybe those gods or creatures or whatever you want to call them, maybe, just maybe, they know better than you do.

ASHANTI: But maybe they don't. Age doesn't always equal wisdom. Isn't that exactly what you were saying about the way our parents destroyed the planet?

EVA: We're talking about a whole different scale here.

ASHANTI: That doesn't matter. I have to listen to my instinct - to what feels right. And this just feels fundamentally wrong to me. I'm sorry.

(ASHANTI *shakes her head and looks down.* EVA *looks frantically at* DAD/CERNUNNOS. *He makes a "go on" gesture to her.* EVA *hesitates.* DAD/CERNUNNOS *makes a "come on already" gesture.* EVA *sighs.*)

EVA: Do...do you remember how good it felt when we looking at the crystals on the altar the other day?

(ASHANTI *looks up.*)

ASHANTI: That might as well have been a thousand years ago.

(EVA *picks up a clear crystal from the altar.*)

EVA: Remember what this one was called?

(EVA *drops the crystal in* ASHANTI's *hand.*)

ASHANTI: The ice of eternity....

EVA: That feeling we had together. It was pure and it was beautiful and it was healing. You can't deny that. And that energy, that literal spark between us, that's what made Cernunnos cross into this plane of existence and made everything else possible.

(A low humming can be heard in the air. It's the same low humming we heard the last time EVA *and* ASHANTI *handled the crystals.)*

ASHANTI: I do feel…something…it's so…strange….

*(*DAD/CERNUNNOS *holds out his palm towards the altar, and softly murmurs words to himself that we cannot clearly hear.)*

EVA: This whole thing started with love. I know the cost is high. But doesn't that energy, that spirit, that cocoon of love make it fundamentally right on some deeper level?

(The humming gets louder. DAD/CERNUNNOS *continues his murmuring.)*

ASHANTI: Maybe…maybe you're right.

EVA: You feel your heart softening to what we have to do, don't you?

ASHANTI: I think I do. I feel my heart softening.

EVA: Your desire to join in the sacred ritual is cresting.

ASHANTI: My desire to join in the sacred ritual is cresting.

EVA: The ancient, um…wait…the ancient ways?

DAD/CERNUNNOS: *(Whispering)* Path…

EVA: The ancient bath? That doesn't make sense….

DAD/CERNUNNOS: *(Louder)* Path. Ancient path…

*(*ASHANTI *cocks her head.)*

ASHANTI: What…?

*(*ASHANTI *looks behind her, and sees* DAD/CERNUNNOS *with his hand stretched out to the altar He quickly drops it.)*

EVA: Uh-oh.

(The humming in the air abruptly stops.)

ASHANTI: What's going on…?

DAD/CERNUNNOS: Like I said, sex magic is the most powerful of all the magics. It creates a conduit in which all manner of things are possible. Like manifesting me. Or…

ASHANTI: Or what…?

DAD/CERNUNNOS: A certain kind of persuasion, shall we say.

ASHANTI: Mind control? You were trying to do mind control on me?!?!

EVA: It's not mind control. It's absolutely not! The spell just focuses your heart towards one aspect of yourself. I can't make you think anything you weren't already thinking or feeling on some level. We were just… guiding you.

ASHANTI: You mean manipulating me.

EVA: Don't you get it? The fact that it worked at all means that on some level, deep down, you do think I'm right. All we did was put a spotlight on something that was already there.

ASHANTI: No. No! Aside from all the other disturbing things going on here, you violated me. We're done. Not only am I not doing your awful, homicidal ritual, but I am never, ever speaking to you again.

EVA: Ash, please…

(ASHANTI *ignores* EVA *and goes back towards the coat rack.* DAD/CERNUNNOS *looks at* EVA *and nods.* EVA *closes her eyes, sighs, and nods. As* ASHANTI *takes her protective gear off the rack,* EVA *picks up one of the plant stands that formed the perimeter of the magic circle earlier in the play. It's big, and heavy.*)

EVA: I'm sorry, Ashanti.

(ASHANTI *doesn't turn around.*)

ASHANTI: Don't waste your breath.

EVA: This whole thing is just so much bigger than you.

(EVA *heaves up the plant stand. She struggles for a moment, until* DAD/CERNUNNOS *gestures with his hand, magically enhancing* EVA*'s strength. With one swift movement, she knocks* ASHANTI *across the back of the head.* ASHANTI *crumples to the floor.)*

EVA: You're sure this is still going to work?

DAD/CERNUNNOS: Like I said, I can spare at least one voice. All I need is her body.

(Pause)

EVA: Think she'll ever forgive me?

DAD/CERNUNNOS: I don't know, kiddo. You just have to stay strong knowing that you're doing the right thing. And sometimes doing the right thing means sacrifice.

EVA: No kidding.

DAD/CERNUNNOS: Now come on. Let's finish what we started, huh?

(EVA *nods, and walks to the foot of the stairs.)*

EVA: *(Calling)* Jane! Imogen! Claire! We're ready!

(A moment, then JANE, IMOGEN, *and* CLAIRE *Appear at the top of the stairs. They all see* ASHANTI *at once.)*

CLAIRE: Oh, holy shit.

(The three of them run down the stairs.)

JANE: What did you do, Eva?

CLAIRE: She killed Ashanti. Oh my God…

EVA: I didn't kill her. I just…you know, knocked her out.

IMOGEN: Hey, I get it. I've been dreaming about laying the bitch out for years.

(JANE *feels* ASHANTI'*s pulse, and listens to her breath.*)

JANE: She seems...fine. I guess.

EVA: Yeah, like I told you. Don't you trust me?

JANE: I'm going to go with a hard no there.

IMOGEN: I for one don't trust you, but I respect you - pretty much for the first time ever.

EVA: Jane. Please. It's not like I wanted to. She was going to leave, and that...well that just couldn't happen.

CLAIRE: So what, if we try to leave, are you going to take the rest of us out too?

EVA: Like Dad said, we need as many voices as we can get. Just taking you all out isn't really an option. So... please....

JANE: This is all so fucked up. So very, very fucked up.

EVA: Okay, yeah, fair enough, but you're still doing the ritual, right?

JANE: Is that how you see me? Just...someone who does things for you?

EVA: No. Jane, no. I've always cared so much about what you think.

DAD/CERNUNNOS: Kid, why don't we /focus, and -

JANE: You've never cared about Mom. Or me. Or probably anyone.

EVA: Jane. Your feet are on the ground.

JANE: No.

EVA: Yes. Your feet are on the ground.

DAD/CERNUNNOS: Kids, this feels like a real potential emotional breakthrough for you, but if we could save it for another time...

EVA: Your feet are on the ground, Jane. Your body's in this space.

JANE: You don't get to do that. You don't.

EVA: Please, Jane. Just try / and—

DAD/CERNUNNOS: SILENCE!

(An ominous rumbling sound)

DAD/CERNUNNOS: Now I hate to raise my voice here, kids, but I'm really going to have to insist that we get to the point. We don't have a lot of time here. Either you're going to be a part of this ritual, or you're not.

IMOGEN: Or you're Ash, apparently.

DAD/CERNUNNOS: Everyone who wants to participate, please step into the circle.

(EVA and IMOGEN immediately step into the circle. EVA hesitates, then steps out and drags ASHANTI's motionless body into the circle as well. A moment)

IMOGEN: Claire?

CLAIRE: It's a big decision. Let me think about it for a second.

(IMOGEN steps out of the circle.)

IMOGEN: It's up to you. I'm in if you're in.

(CLAIRE thinks, sighs, then joins the circle, followed by IMOGEN. They all look at JANE.)

EVA: I understand if you never want to speak to me again.

JANE: Oh, I don't plan on it.

EVA: Really? Okay. Well, I accept that.

JANE: Don't you want to see Mom first? Even for a minute?

EVA: Yeah. I do. But that'd be for me, not for her. So what's the point, you know? I'm kind of a lost cause at this point.

JANE: Eva, hey, no. Don't say that. I…

EVA: What?

(JANE *shakes her head, and silently joins the circle.* EVA *lights the candles as the others look at each other uneasily.*)

DAD/CERNUNNOS: Good. Good. All you have to do is hold hands.

(*They do.* EVA *and* IMOGEN, *who flank* ASHANTI, *awkwardly lean down and grasp her limp hands.*)

DAD/CERNUNNOS: And repeat after me.

EVA: Don't we have to cast the magic circle?

DAD/CERNUNNOS: The magic circle is there as the boundary between worlds. We're tearing that boundary down today. Now kids, this part is very important. If this body returns to the grave before the ritual is complete, it's very important that you just keep going.

EVA: Wait. Return to the grave?

DAD/CERNUNNOS: Along with the rest of the adults. Of course.

EVA: But you're…Cernunnos. You're immortal.

DAD/CERNUNNOS: I am Cernunnos, and I will be again. This body, though - it's your father, and it can't stick around. Sorry, Bucky. I thought you knew.

EVA: No…

JANE: NOW you're saying no?

EVA: I thought…I don't know what I thought.

CLAIRE: You thought you'd be the one kid on the planet who got to keep her dad.

EVA: I mean, not the only kid. Teenage pregnancy is still a real problem…

DAD/CERNUNNOS: Eyes on the prize, kiddo. Remember what we said about sacrifice?

EVA: Yeah. Right. Yeah. It's…it's fine. I'm fine. It'll be fine. I'm good.

IMOGEN: You sure? Because I seem to recall that actual murder was on the table with Ash, so it's not like we don't have options here.

EVA: Will you remember me?

DAD/CERNUNNOS: Of course I will. I hold thousands of years of memories.

EVA: I mean…like you do now. As my dad.

DAD/CERNUNNOS: Oh. Well, I'm not going to lie to you, kiddo. Probably not. But that doesn't mean you won't get to remember, right?

EVA: It's not the same.

DAD/CERNUNNOS: No, it's not. But it's not nothing, right?

(EVA *nods her head.*)

EVA: Okay, let's do this.

DAD/CERNUNNOS: Hang on, kids, and don't be scared. There's a beautiful new beginning on the other side of all this.

(*They look at each other apprehensively.*)

DAD/CERNUNNOS: Now, repeat after me…East, West, North, South!

ALL: East, West, North, South!

DAD/CERNUNNOS: By the great power of Cernunnos, we command you.

ALL: By the great power of Cernunnos, we command you.

DAD/CERNUNNOS: Dripping deluge, come and cleanse creation!

ALL: Dripping deluge, come and cleanse creation!

(Sudden, torrential rain pounds against the basement windows.)

DAD/CERNUNNOS: Blazing blades, swing and slice down the sickness!

ALL: Blazing blades, swing and slice down the sickness!

(Thunder boom and lightning flashes. CLAIRE screams.)

IMOGEN: It's okay, Claire. I'm here. I've got you.

EVA: Stay with it…focus everyone…

DAD/CERNUNNOS: Wailing winds, twist and tear away the torments!

ALL: Wailing winds, twist and tear away the torments!

(Howling wind. And now—other sounds too. Sirens. Car alarms. People shouting and screaming in the distance.)

IMOGEN: It's happening. Holy shit. It's really happening.

(A much closer scream, directly above them, that abruptly cuts off.)

JANE: Mom….

EVA: Stay with us, Jane. Don't break the circle. Please. I'm begging you.

DAD/CERNUNNOS: Empowered earth, rise up and roil over your rebukers!

ALL: Empowered earth, rise up and roil over your rebukers!

(The ground rumbles. Wind, rain, thunder, lighting, and the sounds of screaming get louder. The basement windows shatter. Rain and wind whip inside the basement. The candles suddenly flare up, then out.)

EVA: Shit…

(Light returns to the stage as EVA quickly relights the candles. DAD/CERNUNNOS is gone, but for a just a moment, there's a horned shadow on the wall. EVA sighs, and rejoins the circle.)

EVA: Okay, um… Scourge the earth!

ALL: Scourge the earth!

JANE: I feel it…the light…the air…it's changing.

EVA: SCOURGE THE EARTH

ALL: SCOURGE THE EARTH

CLAIRE: Holy crap, my heart's beating so fast….

EVA: And let it emerge reborn!

ALL: And let it emerge reborn!

EVA: Let it emerge reborn!!

ALL: Let it emerge reborn!!

(The sounds of chaos and destruction outside get louder and louder, as the wind and rain in the basement continue.)

IMOGEN: We. Are. Goddeses. Feel our motherfucking power!

EVA: REBORN!

ALL: REBORN!

EVA: REBORN!!

ALL: REBORN!!

EVA: REBOOOORN!!!

ALL: REBOOOORN!!!

(The wind and rain and thunder and lighting and rumbling and screaming crescendo. ASHANTI sits up, opens her eyes, and gasps. The candles blink out again, and everything goes abruptly silent.)

(A moment, then the sound of a bird singing in the darkness as the play ends.)

END OF PLAY

www.ingramcontent.com/pod-product-compliance
Lightning Source LLC
Chambersburg PA
CBHW052209090426
42741CB00010B/2466